WILDFLOWERS

WILDFLOWERS

Seasonal Splendors of the North American West

GRAHAM OSBORNE

INTRODUCTION BY STEPHEN HUME

CHRONICLE BOOKS

SAN FRANCISCO

To my mom and dad, Rose and Ken Osborne,
who helped make it all possible

First published in the United States in 1996 by Chronicle Books

First published in Canada in 1996 by Greystone Books,
a division of Douglas & McIntyre Ltd., Vancouver, B.C.

Library of Congress Cataloging-in-Publication Data available

ISBN 0-8118-0919-6

Editing by Nancy Flight and Maja Grip
Cover design by Julia Hilgard Ritter
Book design by DesignGeist

Printed in Hong Kong
10 9 8 7 6 5 4 3 2 1

Chronicle Books
275 Fifth Street
San Francisco, CA 94103

Contents

Photographer's Preface

The desert air is warm and still, laced with the sweet scent of primrose and lemon blossoms. I slip quietly from my sleeping bag at 4:00 A.M., the eastern horizon aglow with the deep grenadine red promise of sunrise. A jackrabbit scuttles for cover in a pincushion thicket of jumping cholla. Coyotes yip nervously in the foothills as the waning crescent moon fades silently into first light.

I carefully pick my way through a stand of desert cactus to the sandy floodplain of a small desert creek. Here, great patches of showy white evening-primrose, pink sandverbena and desert sunflowers carpet the low, rolling dunes for acres, growing in such abundance that it is almost impossible to take a step without crushing one or more of the delicate blossoms. The bloom this spring is perhaps the finest in fifty years, maybe ever. This is what I have come for, and the scene is a striking one.

The lighting is dramatic, as the first rays of sun spotlight the valley floor. I scramble to set up my 4 x 5 camera in a race against the changing light, squinting hard under the camera's dark cloth and trying to maintain sharpness in both the spectacular foreground flowers and the distant mountains. The process is frustratingly slow. The sweat stings my eyes as I desperately work to squeeze off a couple of frames before the light is gone.

I start the first two-second exposure but yank the film holder out prematurely as two of the big foreground primroses bob and dance impishly in a fickle desert down draft. At $8 a shot, it is an expensive breeze. I hold my breath, hoping this will somehow still the desert thermals.

The wind falls silent for a few seconds, but just as quickly the sun slips behind the clouds and the delicate morning light vanishes. For the next half hour I sit intently staring at the flowers, waiting for that perfect moment as the wind and sun flirt annoyingly with my scene. A large bank of clouds moving in from the west threatens to end everything, but miraculously I am given thirty seconds of grace and I manage two quick shots before the light is gone for good.

This is certainly the penance of a wildflower photographer. Incessant wind, compromised light, erratic weather and inconsistent blooms, often coupled with remote locations, make wildflower imagery one of the most frustrating yet rewarding forms of landscape photography.

Perhaps it is the challenge that draws me to this pursuit, or the sheer beauty of it. Or perhaps it is the excitement of capturing places that surpass human imagination – that truly testify to the work of God's hand on this land. Just to know that such places exist is enough, but to have the opportunity to experience and photograph them is a blessing. It is my hope that we will have the good judgement to protect these fragile ecosystems entrusted to our stewardship and that the images in this book might help contribute to that end.

Graham Osborne

Introduction

Behind me, a wall of darkness. Before me, gleaming in a dwindling light, what the Blackfoot call the Backbone of the World. Sunset had driven a golden wedge between craggy peaks and sullen rain clouds, which settled like sedimentary rock upon the grassy approaches to the Rocky Mountains. These clouds were nothing like the fast-moving thunderheads that erupt from the arid rain shadow at the edge of the western cordillera. The day before, from a bluff above the Belly River, stunted cottonwoods in the bottoms turning up the silver bellies of their leaves on the gusts, I'd watched one of these localized storm cells flail through on spikes of lightning. It towered over the mountains, a black-based pillar of threat flanked by dust devils and, beyond them, tumbleweed outriders that kicked and bounded away to pile up in the corners of distant fence lines. The barbed wire thrummed and moaned in the wind.

The image lingered, an overlay on my present perceptions, a sense of everything on a huge scale, dramatic and alien to the contained geography of my home landscape in the tawny Gulf Islands. There, miniature south-facing meadows among the Garry oaks and arbutus had already rippled with an early bloom. Embroidered with the gold of buttercups and a brocade of rosy sea blush, thick carpets of blue camas herald every coastal spring. Here on the high plains, that blue tint on mountain slopes was not of early flowers but late snows.

The Blackfoot are right. The Rockies are the backbone of the continent. North America's cordillera covers an area roughly the size of western Europe. To the east lies the dismembered, tornado-prone expanse of the Great Plains, carved into wheat fields and cattle pasture and reaching all the domesticated way south to the Gulf of Mexico. Beyond the mountains to the west lies a dry interior plateau dominated by yellow pine and sagebrush. Next come the wild volcanic uplands that form a complex of mountain ranges commanding the coastal skyline from Alaska to Oregon. Farther south, in California, these ranges divide into a wishbone. A colossal intrusion of granite 650 kilometres long and 130 kilometres wide — the Sierra Nevada — rules the eastern side of the state. The Cascades push down the northwestern coast. Between is a great dry valley.

Among the unifying strands that weave this diverse and fractured landscape into a complex, connected web of communities is an astonishing tapestry of wildflowers. Their colours emblazon the murkiest swamps and the most brutal urban cementscapes.

Country roads slice through biotic zones. The margins are colonized by aggressive newcomers like butter-and-eggs, a pretty visitor from Europe resembling a slender yellow snapdragon. Yellow-flag escapes to moist ditch bottoms from urban gardens. And new avenues of light encourage native species like goatsbeard, its lacy white flowers waving against the dark green forest on standards as tall as a man.

Of course, some floral displays can only be seen with a mountaineering expedition. One must leave the beaten path to spy dense mats of bunchberry, or the flame-coloured trumpets of honeysuckle, or mountain rhododendron, radiant in the gloomy understorey.

Wildflowers bloom somewhere upon this crumpled edge of the continent in every month. A few thrust bravely into the world before the last frosts have ceased. Primroses and periwinkle brighten the dark woods around my house in January. Others come in a rush of spring colour, a lambent fire banishing drabness from the landscape. A second flush rules the late summer and early fall, perfuming the mellow air. Small wonder that wildflowers populate our literary, aesthetic and spiritual imaginations as no other living things do.

We choose flowers to represent our own most fragile and sensitive emotions. They serve as metaphors for the fleeting time we are granted to appreciate the important intangibles that enrich our lives. Flowers are associated with the great transitions in life, the awakening of love, acts of creation, arrivals and departures. We codify these feelings into rituals—the funeral wreath, the graduate's corsage, the bouquet for the ballerina, the long-stemmed rose to woo a lover. An archaic "language of flowers" ascribes various feelings to different blooms and permits non-verbal messages of deep emotion. The bride's bouquet is still caught by unmarried women. The wild rose urges simplicity, the white lily speaks to purity, blue violets express faithfulness. What parent is unmoved by a nosegay of daisies, the symbol of innocence, from a child? Girls today string garlands of spring wildflowers in the fashion of Sappho, who 2,600 years ago told her beloved daughter, Cleis, that "a girl whose hair is yellower than torchlight should wear no headdress but fresh flowers."

Xochitl is the Mexican word for flower. Xochipilli, the Flower Prince, the god of beauty, love and youth, was one of the powerful deities in the Aztec pantheon. The flower-filled terraces of Montezuma rivalled the hanging gardens of Babylon. Their beauty gave even the conquistadores pause. In captivity, Montezuma begged only one thing of his Spanish captors, permission to visit his gardens, and this was granted before he was slain.

Farther north, Salish peoples believed that we are part of the earth and it is part of us and "the perfumed flowers are our sisters." We have been intimately involved with the spiritual symbolism of flowers since that "awakening of awe" in the late Palaeolithic was identified by mythologist Joseph Campbell. That awakening drew an intellectual boundary as concrete as the Rocky Mountains between our most primitive origins and the expression of spiritual awareness that we accept as characterizing full humanity. The Neanderthals first reverently laid a dead family into a grave strewn with wild petals perhaps 60,000 years ago. At the site known as Shanidar IV, an infant, two women and a man were buried on a bier of evergreen boughs, surrounded by blooms of yarrow, cornflower, thistle, ragwort, horsetail and hollyhock — all flowers, incidentally, considered to have strong medicinal value in folk traditions.

Aboriginal peoples from Mexico to Alaska have traditionally used flowers for culinary and medicinal purposes. The ubiquitous western trillium served as an aphrodisiac. The Makah pounded the root and rubbed it on the body as love medicine; a Quinault woman would drop a piece of root into the food of a man she wished to desire her. Among the Thompson, Native healers use trillium for sore eyes and prefer crimson columbine for love potions. Washington's Nez Percé used snowberry decoctions for morning sickness and menstrual cramps. The Chehalis used the same showy white berries for shampoo. Modern herbalists report that wounds treated with snowberry poultices heal with little scabbing. Across the Pacific Northwest, the large leaves of skunk cabbage are still called Indian wax paper after their usefulness in lining berry baskets. The roots were sometimes roasted and ground into a hot, gingery flour. With its fleshy green leaves forming enormous fans against the muddy ground, skunk cabbage has a vaguely tropical look, perhaps because it is related to the taro, the staple food of Polynesian peoples.

Almost every flowering plant seen in the West in some way affected Native life. When ethnologist John Hellson and botanist Morgan Gadd teamed up more than twenty-five years ago to look at this aspect of aboriginal culture, they found a host of ceremonial uses intended to place a person in the appropriate condition to receive power from the sacred realm. Among the Blackfoot, smudge from the yellow balsamroot cleansed the place in which a sick person lay. Inhaled, it was a treatment for headaches. Spread on the body, it increased the ability of runners herding buffalo into slaughtering pounds before the horse rendered them obsolete. Farther west, in the Kootenay River grasslands and the open sagebrush of the Columbia and Okanogan River basins, its tuberous root was a prized food.

The World Health Organization points out that today 80 per cent of the world's population relies on traditional folk remedies. More than 80,000 medicinal plants are documented throughout the world. Across the western cordillera, it is estimated that 20 per cent of the plants and many of the wildflowers had some culinary or medicinal use in the aboriginal community. Researcher Peter Duisberg discovered that among the Cahuilla of desert California, creosote was used as frequently as we use penicillin. The brightly flowering wild gourds of

California and Mexico were widely used by the Pima, Papago, Apache, Acoma and Laguna peoples to treat everything from hemorrhoids to saddle sores. Mexico even has the Institute for the Study of Medicinal Plants, acknowledgement of the value of ancient wisdom once dismissed by a world culture that alienates itself from nature.

Hellson and Gadd discovered that the power in aboriginal rites did not reside in songs and rituals, as many "literate" European ethnologists had assumed. The power derived from the painting of faces, from the transformation of the commonplace with the application of colour. This, too, has ancient roots. People of the Old Stone Age painted the bodies of their dead with red ochre patterns similar to those used by Blackfoot women after childbirth. In the modern world, women's clothing mimics floral displays, and perfumes derived from floral essences are used to enhance their sexual attractiveness. In the most basic sense, this connects us directly to the natural world's celebration of fertility and the announcement of reproductive cycles that the riotous profusion of wildflowers represents, for it is the organs of regeneration that most appeal to our aesthetic sense.

The wonder of wildflowers — and perhaps the biggest danger to them — is that they bring endless enjoyment to rich and poor alike but have no economic value. Since their value is intangible and their presence transitory, the landscapes that best sustain their interlocked communities are easily sacrificed on the altars of greed and materialism.

For all its apparent fecundity, the western cordillera bears only a fraction of the 250,000 species of flowering plants on the earth. Just over a thousand flowering species are found in the state of Washington. Only 792 species and subspecies of flowering plants are listed in Lewis J. Clark's magnum opus, *Wild Flowers of British Columbia*. All are ephemeral, many are fragile, and too many are endangered, some on a massive scale as habitats disappear in the onslaught of industry and population growth.

It seems odd to think of endangered flowers, since they permeate our awareness of the natural world. Yet the Centre for Plant Conservation believes that 1 in every 5 of the 20,000 plant species in the United States is at risk from habitat loss, livestock predation and commercial exploitation. Perhaps 700 species are in imminent danger of extinction over the next ten years. Arizona cliffrose, San Diego button-celery, Sonoma spineflower, California jewelflower, San Joaquin woolly threads, scrub lupine and Macoun's meadow-foam are a few of those in danger of becoming memories extracted from museum photographs.

The encroachment of development on habitats has helped force more than one hundred species of British Columbia plants onto the endangered species list. Another three hundred are considered "threatened." Hundreds more are "vulnerable." The majority of these species, like the golden Indian-paintbrush and Macoun's meadow-foam, are found on the fragile east coast of Vancouver Island. There are now only ten known locations of golden Indian-paintbrush in Oregon and Washington. This remarkable parasitic flower blooms in the open areas most desired for residential building sites. In British Columbia its range is reduced to two tiny, uninhabited islets off Vancouver Island. The fate of Macoun's meadow-foam is even more precarious. It is known only from a handful of populations in British Columbia and does not exist anywhere else in the world.

How quickly we forgot Chief Seattle's plea that we "keep the land apart and sacred, a place where we might go to renew the spirit and taste the wind that is sweetened by the meadow flowers."

The floral zones sweetening the wind of the western cordillera are chiefly classified according to botanical community, by geo-climatic region or by altitude.

Botanically, three groups of flowering plants dominate. One advances from the northern circumpolar realm, expanding southward from Alaska and the Yukon Territory along mountain ridges, where the elevations create climatic conditions similar to those in northern latitudes. Another group is the exotic remnant of plants that colonized North America after migrating from Asia during the last ice age. A third group invades from the south as glaciers retreat, colonizing the south- and west-facing slopes.

Underlying geologic structures determine the great divisions of natural geography: the Rocky Mountains, the dry plateau between the Rockies and the coastal ranges, the Great Basin to the south, a southwestern tongue of desert, California's Great Central Valley, the Pacific Northwest and its coastal lowlands.

The Rocky Mountain region is an area rich in colourful annuals and perennials. Here's where the high country hiker finds alpine meadows vivid with cinquefoil and skyrocket, bee-plant and elephant's-head, Mariposa and old-man's-whiskers, mountain heliotrope and the ragworts, groundsels and buttercups. The intermontane plateau is populated by thrifty buckwheats, phloxes, brown-eyed Susans and Oregon sunshine. The arid Great Basin between California's Sierra Nevada, the southern end of the Cascade Range and the Rocky Mountains supports desert poppy, lupines, sego lily, feathery yellow rabbit-brush and many species of sage — the purple sage that extends from California into the desert valleys of southern British Columbia being most conspicuous.

Desert intrudes into California's southeastern quadrant. It is characterized by plants that have adapted to the extremes of temperature and the shortage of precipitation. This is the land of the creosote bush and the crucifixion thorn. But even here, a sudden spring rain brings forth a forest of ghost flowers, desert trumpets, primroses and devil's claw. The south central coast and lands extending eastward to the Sierra Nevada provide another distinct floral zone. Here in the Great Central Valley, the climate is temperate but dry in the summer months, with heavy snowpacks on mountain heights yielding meltwater flows in late spring. Along the coast, larkspur, blue-eyed Mary and wild-lilac are common. Inland, despite extensive modification by irrigation agriculture and

urban sprawl, dramatic wildflower displays may still be seen along foothill slopes and at the margins of farmland. Higher in the Sierra Nevada, varieties more common in temperate northern zones are found. Saskatoon berry, chokecherry and mountain ash flower on the hillsides; the columbines and penstemons bloom below them or at higher elevations.

The western slope of coastal ranges, extending from northern California to the Alaska panhandle, is the richest floral region by virtue of its temperate climate and ample moisture. Along the coastal fringe, because of the moderating influence of the sea and the abundant rainfall, spring arrives while the continent's interior remains locked in winter's embrace. The first herald is often the lowly skunk cabbage, a remarkable wildflower that deserves a better reputation than its name affords. Found in half-drowned areas along stream margins, marshy hollows, swamps and bogs where openings in the canopy let in more light, this member of the arum family illuminates the sombre winter woods with a brilliant splash of colour. Not by accident is it called swamp lantern. Even while a February frost grips the surrounding country, the skunk cabbage will shoulder its luminous yellow helmet, or spathe, through the marshy ground to bloom defiantly in the snow. It is able to do this because its furious growth generates enough internal heat to withstand the outside temperature.

Other flowers in this coastal zone include silverweed, pink fawn-lily and the delicate chocolate lily, found along sandy driftwood beaches, on the alluvial fans at stream estuaries and in grassy meadows at the forest edge. On rocky outcrops, mistmaidens cling to crevices, and in the drier microclimate of Puget Sound and the Gulf of Georgia, sea-pink and gumweed flourish, the latter exuding a thick, sticky coating that is an ingenious adaptation for retaining moisture on the rocky archipelago scattered across the arid rain shadow of Washington's Olympic Mountains.

Farther inland, under the forest canopy, flowering plants and shrubs are marvellously adapted to diminished sunlight. Some, like the vanilla leaf, take advantage of the still air to display very large leaves on spindly stems, creating a mini-canopy of their own near ground level. Others, like Indian-pipe and coral-root, adapt to the absence of light — essential to photosynthesis — by living in symbiosis with fungi. They create saprophytic communities to exploit the wealth of decaying vegetation that piles up thickly on the forest floor.

The floral zones also stratify vertically. Alpine regions are home to a surprisingly complex community of primulas, saxifrages, rock-jasmine and poppies. These flowers turn summer meadows into a blinding array of brightly coloured blossoms. Some of the most glorious floral displays can only be found in the wind and ice-scoured wastes above 3000 metres.

Life there is precarious. The harsh environment includes a broad spectrum of hazards from which the life of lower slopes is protected. Surviving requires a remarkable series of adaptations. Intense ultraviolet radiation, extreme variations in temperature, violent winds and deep snow all create specialized threats, which vary from habitat to habitat. Rocks high in silica, for example, heat more slowly than rocks rich in iron or magnesium. Some rocks retain heat longer at night, warming the soil. Flowering alpine plants adapt themselves ferociously to these local conditions.

Many alpine flowers have evolved protection against temperature fluctuations by insulating themselves with a protective coat of hairs that form a dense, felt-like coating on the organs that remain exposed above ground. Just like an astronaut's space suit, their cloak traps a layer of air, creating a thermal cushion where the temperature is maintained halfway between the plant's internal temperature and the temperature in the outside environment.

The silvery sheen on many flowering plants in the high alpine zone is another adaptation designed to reflect damaging solar radiation. Some develop a reddish pigmentation in their branches to absorb solar rays; many protect themselves against harmful ultraviolet radiation by remaining small to minimize exposed surfaces. These plants often respond to environmental threats as a complex, interlocking community. For example, plants in the snow zone will crowd together in thick tufts and mats, trapping air and moderating temperatures to something between the temperature of the ground and that of the surrounding atmosphere. Other plants develop deep, thick, fibrous root systems to take advantage of the crannies in rock faces, successfully clinging to wind-blasted summits.

Perhaps the most striking adaptation of these alpine flowers is the way in which they compensate for the narrowness of their reproductive window. Deep snow accumulates at the highest elevations, remains even after summer begins and falls again early in the autumn. Flowering alpine plants must complete their entire reproductive cycle in a matter of weeks. To do so, they have evolved survival mechanisms that give priority to that opportunity. Sometimes the reproductive sequence actually begins before the snow has melted, leaving plants well advanced when the spring runoff starts and treating the early hiker to the magical sight of flowers bursting through the granular snow. Alpine regions are especially treasured by climbers, botanists and photographers for their spectacular and massive blooms and for the exceptionally striking colours of the flowers themselves. Plants in the high alpine zone are most beautiful precisely because of their strategy of sacrificing overall strength to the formation of reproductive organs, the large, prolific flowers showing on small plants.

As the flowers adapted to this complicated cordilleran landscape reveal, topography is everything. It determines microclimates because it makes its own weather. If the rain-laden winds off the Pacific are the breath of God, the towering mountains of the coast ranges are the lungs of creation. Their slopes shunt fast-moving, water-laden pressure fronts from the Pacific to cooler elevations, where vapour condenses into snow or rain.

Behind these mountains, dry thermals rise like high-speed elevators above sun-baked eastern slopes, attracting sailplane aficionados from around the world. But I had slogged into this prairie on foot, less interested in sporting modernity than a firsthand glimpse of a past that increasingly seems in danger of vanishing, not only from the landscape, but from our own collective awareness.

The Blood Indian reserve is Canada's largest. It dates back to the vision of chiefs bearing names like Seen From Afar and Father of Many Children, Crop Eared Wolf and Many Spotted Horses. It is still the heart of a sun dance ceremony that reaches further into antiquity than human memory on this continent. In this dusty triangle where the Great Plains crowd the Rockies, one may still find some tracts of unfenced prairie perfumed by sweetgrass.

Once, invited to a shaking tent ceremony among the neighboring Peigan, I was seconded to a harried mother who wanted someone to drive her two daughters into the settlement nearby. The community proved remarkably integrated with its powerful surroundings. Widely dispersed houses sailed the prairie like glacial erratics. Instead of cramming themselves into some European street grid — that linear imposition of order and efficiency, the outpost of reason garrisoned against a dangerous wilderness — the Peigan habitation pattern is organic, loose-limbed as a newborn foal, sprawling like the landscape itself. It invites an unmanicured grassland into the settlement, welcomes the apparent chaos of the natural order. Unencumbered by fences, irrigation or the cultivated fields of industrial agriculture that drive so much of the wildness from our natural world, some places still exist where deer and antelope and Indian mustangs are free to drift like cloud shadows across the sea of grass. That was what I had walked into the prairie to witness.

The last light faded, shadows lengthening behind the grass-muffled drumlins and eskers that linger from the last ice age. The glaciers took most of the topsoil. Everywhere the earth shows its bones. Every fifty years or so, the rain lays bare another level of fossil debris from the age of dinosaurs. Technically, this final approach to the western cordillera is what geologists call knob and kettle topography, the outcrops created and stripped by moving ice, the hollows and potholes scoured out by meltwater. It reminds us of the unseen forces against which our own lives, ephemeral as wildflowers, achieve only the briefest flicker of consciousness. In this landscape, the time frames are so enormous that past and present and future seem inadequate concepts. Tropical oceans from before the last ice age left this legacy of bedrock. It proved as pliable as liquid in the grinding of continental plates. Water itself solidified, behaving more like rock than liquid. When it suddenly liquified again, the immense post-glacial torrents reshaped the foundations laid down by ancient seas. Below me, the river murmured in its timeless work of deepening and widening its valley, signifying the unseen forces that work away beneath our tiny fragments of time. Dark already pooled in the coulee bottoms, and the moonless, starless sky robbed the terrain of its features.

In the time before Europeans arrived, a Blackfoot warrior cleansing himself for the great ceremonials would come to this river. He would bathe himself in the purifying water and wipe himself dry with fragrant sage grass. He would be wiping away not just the grime but also his old body and the bad life with which it had been stained. Then, naked, invisible, preparing for the infusion of a new life, he would walk out into the grassland, towards the shining mountains his people still call the Backbone.

How many of us seek the same renewal from our contact with the natural world? How many of our own desires to escape the acrid smog of great cities and "taste the wind that is sweetened by the meadow flowers" are rooted in the same acknowledgement of hidden powers? Why else would the simple wildflower occupy such a central place in the myths we live by, day to day? We know instinctively that we need wild places where we may cleanse our spirits with the treasure that is beyond value in fleeting fields of wildflowers. And we need to immerse ourselves in the intricate minutiae of nature, to turn from the hectic pace of our increasingly frantic lives to contemplate eternity in a windflower's bloom. We need such places even if only a handful of us ever find a way to them each year, even if the best we can do is drive to the edge and look in, contemplating the ageless nature of what we approach and the unknown — perhaps unknowable — possibilities wilderness may yet contain.

Advancing naked into the prairie to be remade, the Blackfoot warrior laid a bed of creeping juniper boughs, perhaps the same kind of bed that was found with the sleepers from the dawn of human time at Shanidar IV. Other boughs he would arch above himself to keep off the bitterest weather. Then he would wait until the scent of the juniper infused his own odourless body. Only when he was one with the fragrance of the flower-filled landscape, one more strand in the great web of life, only then might the Great Spirit come to him.

I made my own camp of ripstop nylon and plastic. In the curve of a south-facing slope, far enough from the bottoms to evade mosquitos, close enough to listen to the wind trembling through drifts of scrub willow and trembling aspen below the river bluffs, I snugged down to the hard ground, spooning hip bones into the hollows I had scooped out earlier, settling my soft and transient flesh, like so many creatures before me, into the old, welcoming sediments of Mother Earth.

Sleep came before the last sliver of light ebbed from the high alpine to the southwest. The rain followed. It was not the drumming vertical torrent of a thunderhead, but a soft, slanting shower. It whispered across the nylon fly. I woke to it, lay in the dark listening to the spatter of raindrops and turned over smooth pebbles of thought in the mingled sounds of river and rain. It came to me that the mountains ahead, a glimmering, buckled wall that runs from Alaska to Mexico, are indeed the defining characteristic of our consciousness in this far western landscape. Have we arrived at a second great awakening, knowing now that we are not gods empowered to change the world without consequence? The huge structures and unlimited distances foster delusions of permanence and inexhaustible bounty when all the evidence speaks to impermanence and instability, to transience and to natural limits. Beneath our feet, the solid earth is a shuddering jigsaw puzzle of transform and subduction faults. Los Angeles has already been torn loose from the North American plate to be carried away northward with the Pacific plate. The towering peaks of the Olympic Peninsula in northwestern Washington were once drowned seamounts, scraped off the Kula and Farallon plates fifty million years ago and then thrusted up into the Cascade Range.

Despite the rain, I drifted back into a deep, dreamless sleep and slept late, not waking until the heat of the mid-morning sun made the tent oppressive. When I rolled out to greet the day, the landscape of the night had been transformed from blank ground to a dazzling palette of colour. Infused with the life-giving rain, it blazed with a host of newly bloomed wildflowers. I stood surrounded by the bright yellow of balsamroot, the pearly hue of pussy-toes, the silky, bluish-purple of prairie crocus, blue and white larkspur, the pink of three-flowered avens and the showy bloom of yellow avens, which resembles nothing so much as tiny roses, the five bright petals spread out flat among the dark green sepals. Here and there were the white, yellow, blue and maroon splashes of windflowers, named for the way in which the wind opens the petals, shakes them out and blows them away. Looking westward across this scene, I tried to imagine what it might look like from space, the blush of colour flickering across a sere panorama and then vanishing almost as swiftly as it appeared in the late spring and early summer.

No hiker with a soul has rounded a mountain outcrop into an alpine meadow in full bloom or crawled from a tent in the high grasslands to find the fields ablaze with wildflowers without uttering a gasp of appreciation. At some mysterious level this fleeting apparition of beauty reminds us of what the Blackfoot warrior understood, that the power to cleanse ourselves lies in the natural world and in our ability to come to terms with its needs in fulfilling our own.

We have many sins of which to cleanse ourselves. Our great-grandparents thought the flower-fed buffalo were countless, but we wiped them from the Great Plains in a single generation. Our grandparents thought the forests that extended from California to Alaska represented riches without end. The woods were vast and filled with limitless wealth. In less than a century we have changed them forever, and communities that grew up plundering the natural beauty that surrounded them now cry bitterly that they face imminent extinction. At the rate of cutting during the 1980s, the poverty was coming anyway. The Amazonian rain forest that so grips the world's imagination has been reduced by about 30 per cent. America's biologically rich rain forest ecosystem in the Pacific Northwest has been reduced by about 90 per cent. Our parents thought the salmon in the western rivers were endless, and in less than fifty years they squandered the resource. What once seemed endless now teeters on the brink of extinction from California to the Alaska panhandle.

Aboriginal peoples have long understood that human beings, too, are part of the complex interlocking of species that creates the full community of life on this small planet. Young Chief, a Cayuse Indian, refused to sign the Walla Walla treaty precisely because it failed to represent and protect the wider circle of creation. Instead of nurturing what we have, we have been plucking at the strands from which our collective fates are woven. We do it with a kind of demented fury. We are enthusiastic participants in the growth that threatens to destroy one-quarter of the species on this planet by the middle of the next century. In North America, at least 500 species have become extinct since Christopher Columbus arrived. A further 109 species were listed as endangered in 1973. Today, 900 species have joined the list, and 3,700 more are feared to be at risk and wait to have the threat to their survival more fully evaluated.

I stood in the wind on the prairie and smelled the wildflowers that seemed to go on forever. Not far from where I stood, the Blackfoot winter count recorded the last coming of the buffalo. Caressed by the perfumed grass, I looked towards the shining Backbone of the World and repeated to myself a warning, one that my own father read to me long ago: "As for man, his days are as grass: as a flower of the field, so he flourisheth. For the wind passeth over it, and it is gone; and the place thereof shall know it no more."

For thousands of years the great flower-fed herds of the spring sustained a whole people, then, in the twinkling of an eye, they were gone, the people cast down. I considered how odd it is to think of wildflowers as endangered species. And then I thought again of what has happened to the Blackfoot in a few short generations and how what seems most secure is most precarious, while what seems permanent and everlasting is often as ephemeral as the bloom in spring. The more like a depleted moonscape we make our only home, the more of our spiritual selves we destroy. I thought then of Chief Seattle's warning that humankind did not weave the web of life but is merely one strand in it, that whatever we do to the web, we do to ourselves.

Stephen Hume

Alpine

A common name belies a sacred heritage. Among the tribes of the Blackfoot confederacy, a sprig of cow-parsnip was an important part of the sun dance ceremony.

Previous page:

Deep-rooted penstemon spread their

rich mauves over an exposed outcrop.

Facing page:

Not one to respect artificial boundaries,

the avalanche lily blooms across the

blue-clad Cascades, a range of mountains

that straddles the British Columbia–

Washington border.

Bursting into sunlight even before

the snows have melted from the high-

lands, avalanche lilies are among the

richest rewards for hikers who venture

beyond the treeline.

Facing page:

A dense bloom

of wildflowers

decorates the

mountain slopes

with a brocade

of lupine, arnica,

Indian-paintbrush

and mountain

heliotrope.

Yellow arnica,

crimson Indian-

paintbrush and

mountain heliotrope

grace these

mountain slopes.

The austere reaches of the high alpine

are briefly alive with colour as plants

devote their energy to producing the

showy, oversized blossoms that ensure

their continuance from one short

summer to the next.

Facing page:

Delicate as a river of mist, a creek of silt-laden meltwater cascades through a fringe of Indian-paintbrush and broad-leaved fireweed.

Surrounded by a torrent of glacial meltwater, alpine fireweed carpets an alluvial islet in a barren land-scape.

First light falls on a field of Indian-paintbrush and pearly-everlasting on the Backbone of the World—the Blackfoot name for the Rocky Mountains.

Facing page:

Mountain heliotrope, lupine, arnica

and Indian-paintbrush dominate a

steep alpine slope.

The blue and white spires of lupines

thrust their way through drifts of

mountain arnica, a hardy mountain

variety adapted to cooler altitudes.

Facing page:

The dwindling light of late evening

highlights the wispy heads of western

pasqueflower, waiting for a breeze to

loft their seeds across the carpet of

fleabanes and Indian-paintbrush below.

Western pasque-

flowers greet the

mountain sunrise

with a feathery

array of seed-

heads.

A constellation of avalanche lilies

shines across the uplands.

*Even where the
glaciers still reign,
the summer sun
brings an explosion
of brilliant broad-
leaved fireweed and
Indian-paintbrush.*

Facing page:

*The little red faces of great purple
monkey-flower, named for its petals'
resemblance to a monkey's face, signal
the presence of a mountainside spring
seep. Monkey-flower provided salad
greens for indigenous peoples and
early settlers.*

Arrayed on a south-facing slope that

catches the early sun, mountain heliotrope,

pasqueflowers, lupines and Indian-

paintbrush texture alpine meadows with

the intricate detail of a Persian carpet.

Fluffy white heads of cotton-grass nod in the breeze that will carry away their airborne seeds.

Facing page:

Flowers of fleabane, often called daisies but more closely related to sunflowers, vie with arnica and Indian-paintbrush as the spring bloom reaches its zenith in this rich alpine meadow.

The brilliant colours of ground cover and fallen wetland sedges signal the arrival of fall in the alpine zone, but these pearly-everlasting cling tenaciously to their Indian summer bloom.

Mount Rainier

provides a majestic

backdrop to a palette

of lupines and

Indian-paintbrush.

A flower-filled habitat of Indian-paintbrush, mountain heliotropes and arnica.

Desert/ Interior

In a landscape shaped by rain, the rich green texture of grasses softens the eroded contours of a runoff gully while gleaming blossoms along the slopes catch the sunlight.

Wreathed with mist from a heavy spring rain, this sandy wash suddenly teems with evening-primrose, desert-sunflower and desert sandverbena.

Facing page:

As round and bristly as fairytale

hedgehogs, a cluster of barrel cactus

prepares to explode into bright yellow

blooms among a fringe of more

delicate wildflowers.

Barrel cactus

bursts into exu-

berant bloom to

greet the spring

rains.

Previous page:

Open grasslands are ablaze with the

variegated hues of owl-clover and lupine.

Facing page:

Blue lupines and Mexican gold poppies

weave threads of colour through the

tawny grasslands.

Lupines were once cultivated by the

ancient Egyptians for food and hailed

by the Romans for their digestibility.

Facing page:

The stunning blossoms of desert-

dandelions are among the first to

greet the spring in the dry country.

A jumble of tumbleweed brought in on

the wind piles up at the head of a small

desert draw.

Facing page:

A spent thunderstorm shadows the

desert's arid heights as first light gleams

on the white blooms of evening-primrose.

The delicate

tubular flowers

of desert sand-

verbena grace

sandy niches

like this from

the Great Basin

to the Baja.

Austere sticks of ocotillo frame an eerie maze of jumping cholla. The cholla cactus snags on passers-by, bends, breaks off and uses the released tension to propel itself to a new location.

Richer than the treasury of King Midas,

a dense carpet of brilliant yellow

desert blooms illuminates the foothills.

Facing page:

Brittlebush blooms

yellow with all

the suddenness of

the rainbow that

materializes after

a life-giving rain.

A rare display of

desert lilies graces

a badland backdrop

at last light.

This vivid tapestry of poppies,

lupines and owl-clover is almost

blinding in its intensity.

An arc of sunny yellow brittlebush blooms below as the solitary ocotillo shows its distinctive salmon-coloured flowers against the skyline.

Facing page:

Brilliant red chuparosa and yellow brittlebush stain this drab, arid landscape.

Desert asters cling tenuously to a rocky cliffhold along a desert arroyo.

Like the royal purple trim on a high king's golden cape, lupines decorate a field of poppies.

Many members of the enormous sun-

flower family, like this golden beauty,

revel in the desert landscape.

Lupines and poppies predominate among the splashes of colour on the meadows of the intermontane.

Coast

Dense mats of the tough little Farallon weed cling to crevices on the rocky coast-lines of the remote California seabird islands from which it takes its name.

The pale velvet petals of fawn-lilies

provide a delicate garland of colour on

the cape of greens draping this hanging,

mist-fed grotto.

California poppies flame across a

meadow. The Costanoan people believed

that a few flowers beneath the bed

would put any wakeful child to sleep.

Facing page:

Showy bunchberry mimics its close

cousin, the flowering dogwood. The

white "petals" are actually bracts,

or modified leaves. The true flowers

are the tiny, rather dowdy clusters

at the centre.

Ephemeral, almost translucent,

the ghostly phantom-orchid is one

of North America's rarest flowers.

White and red mountain-heathers

sweep through a temperate old-growth

watershed near its confluence with

the Pacific Ocean.

Facing page:

A motif of absolute
tranquillity adorns
the mirror-like
surface of a remote
coastal lake.

The golden chalice
of a yellow pond
lily blazes amid
emerald fronds.

Exposed to cruel winds and salt-laced

spindrift, ice plants huddle together

in mats, an ingenious adaptation to

a harsh seaside environment.

Clustered beside an icy alpine stream,

mauve spires of lupine echo the blush of

a wilderness sunset.

Punctuated by oxeye-daisies, these foxgloves make a forest of vivid exclamation marks.

Facing page:

Delicate as pixies' helmets, the star-shaped blooms of pink fawn-lilies unfold to illuminate the green gloom of an old-growth rain forest.

A spiky crown of sedge adorns a tangle of foxgloves and daisies.

Facing page:

A crisp white splash of

Pacific dogwood.

The ubiquitous Indian-paintbrush

illuminates the western landscape

from the Great Plains to the Pacific

and from Alaska to Mexico. There

are thirty kinds of paintbrush,

many of them parasitic.

Blue common camas and yellow western buttercups lie in a meadow beneath the gnarled branches of Garry oaks in a rare and fragile ecosystem.

Appendix:
Some Common Wildflowers of the North American West

	COMMON NAME	SCIENTIFIC NAME	DISTRIBUTION
Alpine	Arnica	*Arnica* sp.	Many *Arnica* species occur throughout western North America.
	Avalanche lily	*Erythronium montanum*	Ranges from southern B.C. to northern Oregon.
	Broad-leaved fireweed, or river beauty	*Epilobium latifolium*	Ranges from the mountains of western North America south to Oregon and Colorado.
	Cotton-grass	*Eriophorum* sp.	Occurs in wet, cool habitats throughout western North America to central California.
	Cow-parsnip	*Heracleum lanatum*	Occurs throughout western North America.
	Fleabane	*Erigeron* sp.	Numerous species occur throughout western North America.
	Great purple monkey-flower, or Lewis's monkey-flower	*Mimulus lewisii*	Occurs in the mountains of western North America.
	Indian-paintbrush	*Castilleja* sp.	Many *Castilleja* species occur throughout western North America.
	Lupine	*Lupinus* sp.	Occurs throughout western North America.
	Mountain arnica	*Arnica latifolia*	Ranges from Alaska to California and Colorado.
	Mountain heliotrope	*Valeriana sitchensis*	Occurs in the mountains of western North America.
	Pearly-everlasting	*Anaphalis margaritacea*	Occurs throughout western North America.
	Penstemon	*Penstemon* sp.	Various penstemons, or beardtongues, occur throughout the mountains and lowlands of western North America.
	Western pasqueflower	*Anemone occidentalis*	Ranges from British Columbia south to California and east to Alberta and Montana.
Desert/ Interior	Barrel cactus	*Ferocactus* sp.	Occurs throughout the deserts of the U.S. southwest.
	Desert-dandelion	*Malacothrix* sp.	Occurs in the southern half of western North America.
	Desert sandverbena	*Abronia villosa*	Occurs in the southwestern U.S.
	Desert-sunflower	*Geraea canescens*	Occurs in the southwestern U.S. north to Utah.

COMMON NAME	SCIENTIFIC NAME	DISTRIBUTION
Evening-primrose	*Oenothera* sp.	Grows in many habitats in the southern half of western North America.
Jumping cholla	*Opuntia bigelovii*	Ranges from southeastern California to western Arizona.
Mexican gold poppy	*Eschscholtzia mexicana*	Ranges from southeastern California to western Texas.
Ocotillo	*Fouquieria splendens*	Ranges from southeastern California to western Texas.
Owl-clover	*Orthocarpus purpurascens*	Ranges from southern California to western Arizona.
Tumbleweed	*Amaranthus albus*	Ranges from mid- to southwestern North America.

Coast

COMMON NAME	SCIENTIFIC NAME	DISTRIBUTION
Bunchberry	*Cornus canadensis*	Ranges from Alaska to California and New Mexico.
Common camas	*Camassia quamash*	Ranges from southern B.C. and Alberta to Utah and California.
Fawn-lily	*Erythronium oregonum*	Occurs on the coast from B.C. to Oregon.
Foxglove	*Digitalis purpurea*	Occurs mostly along the coast of western North America.
Gold poppy	*Eschscholtzia californica*	Occurs along the coast from southern B.C. to southern California.
Ice plant	*Mesembryanthemum edule*	Occurs along the California coast.
Oxeye-daisy	*Chrysanthemum leucanthemum*	Occurs throughout western North America.
Pacific dogwood	*Cornus nuttallii*	Ranges from southern B.C. to southern California east to Idaho.
Phantom-orchid	*Eburophyton austiniae*	Ranges from southern B.C. to California.
Pink fawn-lily	*Erythronium revolutum*	Ranges from southern B.C. to northwestern California.
Red mountain-heather	*Phyllodoce empetriformis*	Occurs throughout western North America.
Sedge	*Carex* sp.	Many species of sedges grow in many environments in western North America.
Western buttercup	*Ranunculus occidentalis*	Occurs mostly along the coast of Alaska to California.
Yellow pond lily	*Nuphar polysepalum*	Occurs throughout western North America.
White mountain-heather	*Cassiope* sp.	Occurs throughout western North America.

Acknowledgements

A special thanks to my mom and dad, Rose and Ken Osborne. Without their love, support and encouragement, I wouldn't have been able to do this book. Also, thanks to my mom for all the long hours helping out in the office; they are much appreciated. To my grandma, Rozalia Garbier, for being the best grandma in the world. To Karl Spreitz, who helped get me started, and to Bryan McGill and all the staff at *Beautiful British Columbia* for their great support of my photography over the years. To the B.C. government for the Kitlope assignment and help with logistics and photographs. To Rob Sanders, for his continued belief in my photography, and to the production staff at Greystone Books/Douglas & McIntyre for their excellent work. To Nancy Flight, the editor of this book, and Gabriele Proctor, the designer, for helping to make this book an enjoyable experience. To the crew at Pentax for great professional and technical support. And to Richard Hebda, Adjunct Associate Professor, Department of Biology, School of Earth and Ocean Sciences, University of Victoria, for reviewing the manuscript and compiling the Appendix.

A very special thanks to the staff at CustomColor, the best photo lab I have ever used, for unmatched processing, quality and service. In particular, to Paul Good, for unerring processing above and beyond the call, to Kerith, George, Julie, the two Tinas and Mike for all their help and especially to Kate Tully, for exceptional professional service and true friendship over the years. And to all my friends and family, who make it good to come home after the long road trips. Finally, I thank God for keeping me safe and giving me the opportunity and ability to photograph some of the most treasured places on this earth.